BOSS LADIES OF SPORT

PHILLIP MARSDEN

LOTHIAN
Children's Books

I was watching the Tokyo Olympics and seeing all these amazing women who not only excelled as athletes, but whose personality and efforts outside of their sport also shone so brightly. This got me thinking about all the other amazing sportswomen competing in their fields today and although I am the least sporty person myself, I thought I could use the thing that I am good at, drawing, to shout out and celebrate these amazing women – and *Boss Ladies of Sport* was born! I hope you see some of your heroes in this book and that they inspire you to work hard at what you love, to be yourself, and to celebrate all the other boss ladies in your life!

FROM THE AUTHOR

ARIARNE TITMUS

Ariarne, aka 'Arnie', aka 'The Terminator', is a world-champion swimmer in the 200 metre and 400 metre freestyle. She swims a LOT, and to relax she likes to try out experimental recipes and spend time with her family in Australia.

ASH BARTY

It's never over until we're shaking hands at the net. Then you've either won or you've lost and - either way - you look them in the eye and say, 'Well played, mate.'

Like her hero, boss lady Evonne Goolagong Cawley, Ngarigo woman Ash Barty is an Australian tennis superstar. She has won both the French Open and Wimbledon and is currently ranked Number 1 in the world!

BEATRICE 'BEBE' VIO

Bebe (which means 'baby' in Italian) started fencing when she was just 5 years old. When she was 11, she lost her arms and legs to an infection called meningitis, but that didn't stop her! She retrained as a wheelchair fencer with prosthetic limbs and went on to win gold at the 2016 Olympics.

CHARLOTTE WORTHINGTON

Charlotte is a **BMX** Freestyle gold medallist from the United Kingdom and the first woman ever to land the breathtaking 360° backflip in professional competition. **Just wow!**

ELAINE THOMPSON-HERAH

Disappointment makes you better and stronger. I have learnt how to use the disappointment to motivate me, keep working hard and getting better.

Jamaican athlete Elaine Thompson-Herah is the fastest woman in the world!
And the only one to ever do the double-double – winning the gold medal in both the
100 metre and 200 metre races in two consecutive Olympic Games. Catch her if you can!

ELLYSE PERRY

Soccer or cricket? Why not both? This boss lady is the youngest Australian to play international cricket and the first to have appeared in both International Cricket Council and FIFA World Cups. Ellyse, is there anything you can't do?!

FAITH KIPYEGON

No female athlete runs the 1500 metres faster than Kenyan runner Faith Kipyegon.
She won gold at the Rio Olympics in 2016 and Tokyo 2020, and gave birth
to her first child in between. Boss Mum!

JADE JONES

When I was younger and I'd not won anything, it was literally like, you've got nothing to lose, you just go in to win!

Jade is a taekwondo champ from Wales in the United Kingdom. She has won two Olympic golds, along with World and European championships. Her nickname is 'The Headhunter' because she tries to kick her opponents in the head for more points! Look out!

JANJA GARNBRET

The best of the best in female competitive climbing, this Slovenian Spider-Woman won the gold medal the first time sports climbing was featured in the Olympics!

JESS FOX

Remember that it's about progress, not perfection, and that it's more important to try your best and learn from your mistakes to improve for next time.

Daughter of two Olympic canoeists, Aussie Jess specialises in the kayak slalom. She campaigned to have women's canoe slalom added to the Olympics to ensure an equal number of events for men and women, and won gold when the first event was held at the Tokyo Olympics.

JEWELL LOYD

That's the core of it: getting people not to think, 'Wow, here's a woman who can dunk,' but instead, 'Wow, this is a great athlete.'

Jewell's nickname is 'Gold Mamba' (a mamba is a type of snake) because she's deadly on the basketball court. She has dyslexia and works to promote inclusion for people with learning disabilities. The American has won two WNBA championships, a World Cup and an Olympic gold medal.

KATIE LEDECKY

American Katie Ledecky has the most medals of any female swimmer, ever, and holds multiple world records. If that isn't enough, she also has a degree in psychology and political science, and runs a STEM program empowering young girls through education. Crikey!

KAYLEE MCKEOWN

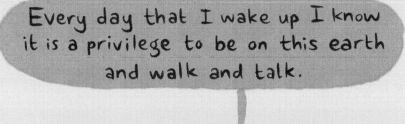

Backstroke queen Kaylee won gold medals in the 100 metres and 200 metres. She also broke the world record for the 100 metres in the Tokyo Olympic trials and dedicated the win to her late father. Her excitement and enthusiasm captured the hearts of all her Aussie fans.

LISA CARRINGTON

Māori canoeist of Te Aitanga-a-Māhaki and Ngāti Porou descent, Lisa is New Zealand's most successful Olympian, having wrapped her impressive guns around 5 gold medals 1 bronze, and numerous world championships.

MADISON DE ROZARIO

Madison is an Australian wheelchair sprinter who has won marathons, world championships, Olympic silver and broken world records. She has spoken out against abuse on social media and promotes body positivity. She has even had a Barbie doll made of her!

MEGAN RAPINOE

Growing up, I was never the best athlete or the fastest or the strongest – so I had to affect the game in a different way.

Megan has won Olympic gold and two World Cups with the USA national soccer team. She campaigns for equal pay for women, protests against racism and is an ambassador for LGBT+ rights. Mic drop!

MOMIJI NISHIYA

Skateboarding is fun and interesting to do, so I want everyone to try skateboarding.

Japan's Momiji Nishiya is the first ever women's street skateboarding Olympic gold medallist . . . at 13 years old! Enough said.

NAOMI OSAKA

Four-time Grand Slam tennis champion from Japan, with a serve faster than 200 kilometres per hour, a prominent Black Lives Matter activist, and one of the highest earning female athletes of all time (ka-ching!). Naomi has taken time out to prioritise her mental health and become an even more powerful role model in the process.

PERUTH CHEMUTAI

Uganda's first ever female Olympic medal winner, and no less than
GOLD in the 3000-metre steeplechase. Boom!

QUAN HONGCHAN

At just 14 years old, Quan Hongchan won Olympic gold for China in the 10-metre platform diving at Tokyo 2020, earning a perfect score of 10 on not one but two of her dives! She also loves snacks and wants to open her own supermarket.

RUBY TUI

Ruby is a prop in New Zealand's Olympic gold medal and World Cup-winning rugby sevens team, The Black Ferns. Her media interviews are a masterclass in enthusiasm, respect and fun!

SAM KERR

The all-time leading goal scorer in the Australian and American women's soccer leagues,
Aussie Sam plays for Chelsea in England and for Australia on the world stage.
She's a fearsome leader and can do a mean backflip!

SIMONE BILES

It's important to teach our female youth that it's OK to say, 'Yes, I am good at this,' and you don't hold back.

Not only is American Simone the absolute GOAT (Greatest Of All Time) of women's gymnastics, but she is also a role model for another type of strength, in stepping off the world stage at the 2020 Tokyo Olympics for the sake of her physical and mental health.

STEPHANIE GILMORE

Stephanie is a seven-time world champion of surfing from Australia.
She has campaigned for equal pay for professional female surfers, is an
advocate for ocean health, and can totally shred on the guitar!

SUSANA RODRIGUEZ

When you love something, you don't care about the effort you put on it or how hard it is, you just go for it.

Born visually impaired due to albinism, Susana is a paralympic triathlete - that's swimming, cycling and running, with assistance from a guide. She's also the first legally blind woman to become a doctor in her native Spain, where she helped out on the front lines against the COVID-19 pandemic!

TALIQUA CLANCY AND MARIAFE ARTACHO DEL SOLAR

We just keep working our way and just getting a little bit better every day.

Nerves are normal, but you try to turn them into positive fire, excitement.

These beach volleyball players are a powerful symbol of strength in diversity. Taliqua is an Indigenous Australian woman from Wulli Wulli and Goreng Goreng country and Mariafe's family emigrated to Australia from Peru when she was 11. They make a great team and together won the silver medal at the 2020 Tokyo Olympics.

VENUS AND SERENA WILLIAMS

These two legendary tennis greats from America take 'sibling rivalry' to a whole new level! They have won a whopping 30 Grand Slam singles titles between them (7 for Venus, 23 for Serena), 14 Grand Slam doubles titles, not to mention Olympic gold medals. They have both been ranked World Number 1, and have even starred in an episode of *The Simpsons!*

YULIMAR ROJAS

The sky is the limit.

Yulimar grew up in rural Venezuela, trying her hand at lots of different sports.
Now she's a world-record-breaking triple jumper, her country's first female
gold medallist, and a proud LGBT+ activist.

YUSRA MARDINI

Flying the flag for refugees - literally and figuratively - as flag bearer for the Refugee Olympic Team in Tokyo 2020, Yusra is a voice and champion for refugees worldwide. In 2015 she escaped the conflict in Syria, swimming alongside a sinking dinghy to steer it to safety in Greece, and later finding asylum in Germany. Now she has swum competitively at two Olympic games!

Dedicated to all the boss ladies who made this book possible

A Lothian Children's Book
Published in Australia and New Zealand in 2021
by Hachette Australia
(an imprint of Hachette Australia Pty Limited)
Level 17, 207 Kent Street, Sydney NSW 2000
www.hachettechildrens.com.au

Text and illustrations copyright © Phillip Marsden 2021

NATIONAL LIBRARY OF AUSTRALIA
A catalogue record for this book is available from the National Library of Australia

ISBN: 978 0 7344 2119 7 (hardback)

Designed by Christabella Designs
Printed in China by 1010 Printing